MY EVOLUTION GUIDE

My Evolution Guide

ALDIVAN TORRES

Canary Of Joy

CONTENTS

1- 1

My Evolution Guide
Aldivan Torres
My Evolution Guide

Author: Aldivan Torres
© 2020-Aldivan Torres
All rights reserved

This book, including all parts, is protected by copyright and may not be reproduced without the permission of the author, resold or transferred.

Aldivan Torres, a native of Brazil, is a consolidated writer in several genres. To date it has titles published in dozens of languages. From an early age, he was always a lover of the art of writing having consolidated a professional career from the second half of 2013. He hopes with his writings to contribute to international culture, arousing the pleasure of reading those who do not yet have the habit. Your mission is to win the hearts of each of your readers. In addition to literature, its main tastes are music, travel, friends, family, and the pleasure of living. "For literature, equality, fraternity, justice, dignity, and honor of the human being always" is his motto.

Book Content
The disease issues

The gift of predicting the future
Loyalty
The critic
The slander
The advice
The dark night of the soul
The consistency of God
Posture towards life
How to be the man of God.
Put yourself in the Other's place.
The power of prayer
How to enter the Kingdom of God.
Tolerance
The role of man
Man's treasure
Being more human
Meekness
The family bases
The incentive
Gratitude
The job of serving the public.
Be yourself
Flirting, dating and marriage.
Caring for yourself
The dignity
The spiritual life
The past of man
The time of god
The true servant of God.
Health professionals
The intrigue
The tramp
The evolution

The friendship
Suffering for love
An attitude of life
The wounded marks
Being an eternal learner
Advertising
Pornography and the trivialization of sex
The value of a human being.
The sublime role of the master.
Greatness in the little things
The pride
Lust
Greediness
Avarice
Will
Vanity
Laziness
Envy
The game
Drugs
Posture at home
The greenhouse effect and its causes.
Trafficking in animals and plants.
Landless movement, without food, homeless, etc.
Capitalism
Plastic surgeries due to vanity
Abortion
Pedophilia
Zoophilia
Incest
Prostitution
Adultery
Sexual Orientations

Scientific research with humans and animals.

The use of stem cells, the use of artificial insemination and in vitro fertilization.

Current public health

Public education

Corruption

Safety

Strike

Live the present

The suicide

Depression

Drug trafficking

Trafficking in persons

Greed

The mission

Recognize yourself a sinner

The spiritual dimensions

The disabled

The value of culture

Do not be afraid

The father and mother as family axes.

Reasonability and proportionality

Despise selfishness

In victory and failure

Be true light

The disease issues

Physical illness is seen by many as punishment for sins, but it should not be seen in this way. It is a natural process indicating that something is not right in our body. Like any other problem, it must be treated with the methods of medicine and once cured, just continue with your daily life as normal.

In case of fatal illness, it remains to take care of the last details of our departure for the eternal kingdom. There, my father will welcome the faithful and put them in the right place. Yes, death is a certainty and let us take care in this world as soon as possible before our spiritual future by doing good works and charity.

"The disease must be seen as a period of inner learning and not as a punishment".

The gift of predicting the future

Being a fortune-teller is an honor and a responsibility to myself, my father and the world. This intriguing special gift allows for premonitions and a certain vision of my future and those I love. It is like a path warning and that I must follow firmly on it. It makes things a lot easier.

However, it is not necessary to be a clairvoyant to know exactly what I must do and what results will be achieved. Everything in this life follows the plant-harvest rule, that is, if you plant wheat, you harvest wheat and if you plant chaff, you will harvest chaff.

Discovering the future little by little and God's love for us is priceless. With every surprise on the way, it is like a balm for the soul. In the end, there remains the certainty that we are what we build and that everything is written because God in his infinite goodness commands everything. Good luck on your projects, brothers.

Loyalty

This is an essential virtue for success in all areas and happiness itself. We need faithful men for our kingdom, who have a convinced faith and who are willing to fight for what they believe. On the contrary, infidels, and fools will suffer for their incessant deviations and errors.

Loyalty is a rare jewel nowadays and whoever has someone like that at their side is the same as earning a great fortune, a wealth that cannot be bought or paid for. With loyalty, they make the human more perfect and worthy for the action of God and his respective forces of good. Blessed be the faithful, their value is incalculable.

The critic

There are two categories of criticism: Constructive criticism and destructive criticism. The first, analyzes its weaknesses and proposes solutions to remedy failures. The latter has the sole intention of judgment to weaken and demotivate him.

Try not to criticize and if you are going to do it, do it intending to help your fellow man and not harming him. Respect the other and his work because nobody owns the truth in this world.

The slander

Live your life in a way that does not care about the opinion of the other, work and live your moments of leisure as if it were alone. If someone's intrigue and lies about you happen to come to your ears, forgive and pray to God for them.

Just do not bow your head due to others and do not give up. Remember that you are a child of God, who like everyone else deserves happiness and success. Don't be moved! Follow and report only to God about your actions.

The advice

All of us, at some point in life, feel doubtful about our path. In these moments, look for someone experienced and reliable to vent and listen to him. Often a good conversation clarifies many facts and gives us a clue where to go.

However, remember that the final decision is in your hands and to do so consider all possibilities. When you decide, do it quickly before you regret it. Only the future will indicate whether the choice was right or wrong. Regardless of the option, what remains are the learning that takes for a lifetime.

The dark night of the soul

The dark night is a period in which the human being falls into darkness, forgetting God and his principles. This moment is the most critical for a human being because he sinks into an intense depression. Now, remember that God is always with you. He is preparing a spacious, clear and sharp terrain, something better than anything he imagined for his life, as he is a father.

After overcoming the Dark Night, focus on your father's love and goals and gradually everything is happening. Never forget what happened or where you left so that the darkness does not torment you again. Repeat with me reader: "Even if I walk through the valley of the shadow of death, I will fear no harm because you are with me." Glory to the father!

If God is for us, who can be against us? (ROM 8.31)

Do not be discouraged by the difficulties, do not care about the obstacles even if they are great. Face your problems head on and show them how great your God is. For if he is in our favor, who can be against him? Furthermore, who is like God?

God, my father, keeps for every human being a surprise and extra talents according to his behavior and need. Everything is written, brothers! So, keep working on your projects with firmness that victory is guaranteed in his name. So be it!

The consistency of God

God is so great that it is difficult to define him in human words. Omnipresent, omniscient and omnipotent God is not a unique being as many thinks, but a legion of supernatural forces for good.

These forces see everything that exists and firmly coordinate the functioning of the universe. Among its main virtues are justice, wisdom, kindness, generosity, understanding, tolerance, peace, power, mercy, fidelity, loyalty, and infinite love for created beings.

I am one of them, and I am the key part of the universe's gear. I was sent to Earth as a peasant to help him evolve and regain his father's lost contact since the arrival of my brother Jesus. I want people to reject the present materialism and embrace my cause, which is just. I want to have them in my kingdom with my father, happy and fulfilled. To achieve that, just follow the commandments, believe in my name and the holy name of the Lord. Blessing and peace to all.

Posture towards life

Life is a big Ferris wheel full of obstacles and difficulties. Everything can be made easier depending on your mental posture. We must have optimistic thoughts and not give up on the first obstacle and failure.

Being optimistic, we will carry other positive thoughts with us and thereby generate new perspectives because man is this: He is everything he thinks and feels. I wish from the bottom of my heart success and peace to all of you in your projects.

How to be the man of God

The man was told to work and care for his father's sheep. Therefore, there is no need to worry about the future, what to eat or drink because the pagans are looking for this. Do you see the lilies of the field? They do not sow and do not plant and yet, their beauty is stunning, greater than the beauty of Solomon with all wisdom and wealth. If God does this with a plant, He will do much more for you, men of little faith.

God specifically cared for each man and woman by caring for their most basic needs. We must seek his kingdom first and the rest will be given to us as an addition, for God is just and good. Blessed be the father forever, amen!

Put yourself in the Other's place.

Do not judge and will not be judged was said to the man. Each case is a situation and for those on the outside it may seem less complicated than it really is. So don't be put off by appearances.

Let each one take care of their problems and go about their lives without looking at the other's. Never point a finger or say that you would do your best. You only know how to be capable in your situation, and it is often best to keep yourself out. Respect your superiors in the family and beyond and contribute in some way to a better country.

The power of prayer

In this world and in the next, man is often subjected to great dangers for the enemies of his salvation. What to do in these critical hours? The power of man is in the power of prayer in which he asks for protection from the higher forces.

Never forget to say your prayers when you wake up and when you sleep. Prayer is a moment of intimacy between the creature and the creator, not having a ready formula. Talk about your life, your problems, ask for thanks, but also give thanks for today. Also ask for your brothers, friends or enemies, so that God gives you a good direction.

In the morning you should pray like this: God the Father, infinite and eternal, I thank you for the opportunity to stay alive and practice your commandments and gifts. I ask that my day and that of my brothers be full of achievements and happiness. I ask for your protection from enemies and wisdom in decisions. I ask for patience and faith in trials. I ask for your enlightenment in all my actions. Anyway, I ask for your blessing, amen.

At night, you should pray like this: Lord God, I ask you for the protection in its entirety. Protect me on the roads and on trips, from assaults; protect me from enemies, that my blood is not spilled; protect me from the evil spirits and their spiritual works, protect me from the infernal entities and powers, from the spiritual beasts, from the spiritual snakes, that the gates of hell do not approach, do not persecute me and do not prevail in my life. Finally, by your blood and your cross, protect me from any category of evil. Amen.

Peace and abundance to all.

How to enter the Kingdom of God

My blessed father and I call you to a kingdom of delights, a kingdom where milk and honey flows. It is open to everyone, but it has some requirements to be met. To enter my kingdom, man has to get rid of the old man and be born again. This is necessary for man to get rid of sin definitively.

Be like children, who firmly believe in my name without further explanation, get rid of stupid rationality. Because not everything has an explanation, and you will only achieve complete happiness in the face of total renewal and surrender. If you really believe that "I am", then the kingdom of God has already arrived for you. However, if you reject me, you will reject the one who sent me and consequently, your future will be compromised. Regardless, I will continue to love you and that is why I have given you free will since the beginning of time. Faith and peace to all!

Tolerance

Behold, I bring the kingdom of God to mankind. However, not everyone is prepared for it. I am looking for faithful men and women of any denomination category and this category of attitude shows my heart and that of my father who calls himself a tolerant. So, I also want my faithful to be.

In the kingdom of God there is no room for prejudice and judgment. They are all children of the same father and have the same rights. Whoever desires greatness, first bow to your brothers and sisters, being the servant of all because the greatest in my kingdom are the little ones. I also have a special predilection for the most humble and generous?

In addition, they are invited to reflect on values and see what category of action they are taking. Remember that your decisions are what will define your special future with your father. So, think hard about what to do and live a world without stereotypes.

The role of man

I am God, king of kings and lord of lords, behold, I created man with the primary purpose of taking care of the planet on which he lives and this includes the protection and coordination of all subordinate beings.

However, I will not allow mistreatment and neglect of what belongs to me. Every sin relates this is written in my book and charged in due time, for I am God, the almighty. I will give glory to those who deserve glory and punish the infidels as they continue to make the same mistakes.

As was said, continue to take care of my vineyard and in due time I will return with the payment deserved for each one. This will be the day of the thief, and it is good that you are prepared. On this day of God, hearts will meet.

Man's treasure

"Do not gather treasures in the land where thieves steal and moths eat away. Rather, gather treasures in the sky where they will be safe. Truly I say to you, wherever your treasure is, there your heart will be."

How to gather this treasure in heaven? First, follow the commandments of the old and new covenants which demand a serious and sober conduct from man. The greatest are to love God above all things, yourself and your neighbor. How can I show this love for my brother? In attitudes and works that benefit the other when he needs it most. It has already been said that charity, in its various forms, redeems sin and magnifies the soul. I still reinforce that those who practice solidarity are one step more evolved than the others and certainly have a glorious future ahead, both on earth and in the spiritual world.

So, brothers, keep helping your neighbor without expecting retribution. God the Father sees everything and will bless you in due time. Follow this chain of good always.

Being more human

The man is the set of two aspects: an animal part, the corporal part, and a spiritual part, the soul. We must develop the two in a way that they are interdependent with a greater emphasis on the spiritual.

From the spiritual side, good vibrations and good acts emanate. With the right preparation, we are able, through the spiritual or human part, to understand exactly what God proposes for our lives and to transform this into concrete acts.

On the contrary, the animal part leads us to weakness and sin. We must cancel it in such a way that it only serves us for survival. As Jesus said, "The spirit is strong, but the flesh is weak."

One way to cultivate healthy spirituality is to engage in social projects, whether reading, community assistance, friends, religious groups, among other things. Good interaction with others causes our ideas to mature and give us a new outlook on life.

Meekness

"Take my judgment on you and learn from me that I am meek and lowly in heart, and I will find rest for your souls".

This phrase from Jesus clearly exemplifies how the faithful must be: meek and humble. By maintaining control and calm, we can convince crowds relates our point of view by avoiding fights or discussions in a dialogue.

There is nothing better in this world than peace with others and with yourself. This sublime sensation is only achieved with the clear application of Jesus' recommendation. The contrary, the lack of control, is the cause of tragedies and violence around the world. Violence does not have to be accepted in the kingdom of God because it breaks the main rule of good coexistence with the brothers and violates the greatest meaning of life: Love. If there is any word that can describe God, it is this. Therefore, always practice meekness, universally, my dear brothers.

The family bases

The family is the first community in which we participate and as such its members have rights and duties. Parents have a great responsibility to train their children, to fill their minds with moral concepts so that they have a good basis for facing life. Children as far as they are concerned must respect the authority of their parents, try in their studies and when young people or adults go on with their life, getting married or entering religious life. In both options, parents should be helped when necessary, especially in old age.

Having a good family base, children will have no problem adapting to society, its rules and growing demands. Parents will be proud and take their teachings to others, perpetuating this cycle of good.

The incentive

Incentive is one of the main ingredients of success. Be sure to support your brothers in your projects even if they seem weird or impossible. The other's indifference causes pain and discouragement.

I am an example of what I have always faced: the incomprehension of others. I confess that it was not easy to manage my impulses, projects and dreams, but I won. I won without the support of any human. Therefore, always encourage your family member or friend, as it is of fundamental importance.

Gratitude

We are all subject to giving and receiving. When you have, the opportunity does not hesitate to help and when you need it do not hesitate to ask or seek the means to get out of the problem.

It is part of human honor and the right attitude not to forget help or the benefactor. This is called gratitude and those who have it keep one of God's commandments. So be happy to give and receive.

The job of serving the public.

You, who work in the public service, have a great mission ahead of you. Do not forget the essential virtues of the attendant: helpfulness, efficiency, understanding, attention, knowledge, and availability. Do the work with dedication by treating others as you would like to be treated. Be patient with the ignorant and violent. Do not react.

The image of the institution depends on the attendant, which must be preserved. Depending on your performance, you are likely to make new friends and win customers for a lifetime. Therefore, consider your work of paramount importance to the financial health of the company or public agency. Always do your work with love and care and be happy.

Be yourself

In the fifth saga of the series the seer, called "Sou", the book presented a memorable lesson relates the aspects of each character experienced in everyday life. Each of those thirteen people of whom twelve were invited to be my apostles had personality problems and were unable to accept or see themselves. The moral of society prevailed in their lives. What does today's society demand of us?

It requires compliance with rules that only target material, financial status, power, political, racial, ethnic and sexual discrimination. The society is divided into groups and the majorities step on top of the minorities. For these and other reasons, these groups add more and more bewildered people.

As in the book "I Am", I reiterate my position and opinion and I am not obliged to agree with the majority. God the Father created man with the necessary freedom to make his own decisions and I believe that the nature must be sacred. Even if social rules allow, I will not go over my ethics and values to get along. I prefer to be the reverse of the majority than to be with a heavy conscience.

"I am" myself and I always will be as long as I live no matter who I face. I am only obliged to comply with the rules imposed by law and extend to all citizens. Aside from that, I am completely free in all situations. So be brothers too.

Flirting, dating and marriage.

A relationship for two to be successful needs to be filled with some essential ingredients. Respect, dialogue, knowledge, friendship, love, patience, tolerance, understanding, and fidelity are the main ones. This is what makes a successful relationship for two extremely rare today.

Most people are individualistic, selfish, and demanding. They prefer not to go back on a decision rather than having to lose their pride. As a result, they often miss the opportunity to be happy.

Flirting and dating should be the moment of knowledge between the two projecting a serious relationship in the future. Most relationships end there because of disagreements or simply because one of the two does not want to commit to a relationship. The latter 'item' is eighty percent of the cases. What is seen is an increase in promiscuity and casual sex harming self-love.

In cases where dating or flirting turns into marriage, a large part ends up separating due to unpreparedness or even routine. It is one thing for you to date each one in your home. Another thing is to be side by side daily, in the sun, rain, clothes to wash, food to do and still have to endure sometimes the bad mood of the other.

My advice is for the partners to get to know each other a lot and test the love because it is the last refuge when the couple's problems tighten. Those who have not yet married, do not be discouraged. For each one there is a soul mate on earth. Congratulations to the married couple on their decision and take care of love as if it were a plant that needs daily care so as not to wither. In addition, loving is too good and God wishes everyone happiness.

Caring for yourself

God created us from the beginning for a life full of harmony and happiness. However, because we are in material form, we are subject to accidents of all kinds and diseases.

What God requires of us is that we take care of our bodies so that major problems are avoided. Take preventive exams at least once a year, protect yourself with condoms and vaccines against opportunistic diseases, taking care when crossing the streets or driving a car. There is little care when your life is at stake.

The dignity

Man's dignity is a rare jewel that has to be carried wherever he goes. How to become worthy before God? First, to strive to have an occupation whatever it may be because vagabonds do not prosper or are happy. Comply with the greatest possible number of commandments of the law of God, fulfill the obligations of citizens, respect the family, yourself, others and have full faith in God.

This range of elements makes man capable of being dignified and ready for the future that awaits him. With other virtues, they build a human being capable of understanding the divine project and achieving success.

The spiritual life

Earthly life is a passing stage of our existence that converges to the spiritual realms. Many wonders: how will we be? What does spiritual life consist of? I will explain these issues.

Spiritual life is the continuation of earthly life. We lose our material body and gain a spiritual one with the same functions. In the new kingdom that we deserve, heaven, hell, or city of men we will perform specific spiritual functions: protection, worship, specific services of the dimension, interaction with other spirits among other activities.

Anyone who thinks we have changed something is wrong. In the spiritual realm, we will be the same as we are on earth, the change is only of consistency, from the material to the spiritual. So, make your current life the bridge to raise higher flights with your father.

The past of man

Was your past dark and does it accuse you? Do you feel guilty and insistently remember your mistakes? This attitude is not healthy and will not get you anywhere. Be aware that you have already changed or are about to change and what happened no longer matters. What matters is the present in which you can build a different future.

Do you remember when Christ forgave the criminal on the cross? He will do the same for you if you cry out for mercy and firmly decide to change. Because for the father everything has been forgotten, and he believes in his dignity and suitability. The father knows you, knows that you are capable and is always willing to understand you. For us, he stretched out on the cross and died. Do not allow this sacrifice to be in vain.

The time of god

"For everything there is a time, for every occupation under the heavens there is a time: a time to be born and a time to die, and a time to uproot what has been planted; time to kill and time to build; time to cry and time to laugh; time to throw stones and time to collect them; time to embrace and time to part; time to seek and time to lose; time to keep and time to throw away; time to tear and time to sew; time to be silent and time to speak; time to love and time to hate; time for war and time for peace. "

This sentence clearly exemplifies that everything happens in due time and at its pace. Therefore, there is no point in lamenting or desperately looking for something, as this is not up to us.

The man plans, but the answer comes from God. He writes the facts to come in crooked lines. It is up to the man to work focused on his goals and put himself at the disposal of the creator because as the saying "Do your part I will help you".

In addition, get on with your life without any major worries. Whatever has to happen will come if it is so written. It is also up to man to accept the divine will in all circumstances because he is always sovereign and wise. Blessed be my father's name!

The true servant of God

As Jesus said, there are many who call him Lord and live in their churches preaching love and peace. However, most do not take this intention into practice and continue to commit the same sins: slander, envy, pride, prejudice, selfishness and other defects. These are those who do not have their names written in the book of life.

The true servant of God is known for his continued discretion and generosity. They are the ones who, when they see a beggar on the street, approach and ask how he is or still answer his calls for help. The faithful servant will follow the commandments of the old and new covenants and are known in the community as examples of good conduct. These will be the first to be resurrected when Jesus comes and will reign with him forever, as we receive exactly what we deserve.

There is still time for you to make a difference and join the chain of good. Do it right away, don't delay what can be done today. My father and I will bless you and cover you with graces throughout your life.

Health professionals

You, who work in the health services who are a doctor, nurse, technician or nursing assistant, cleaning or reception, among other functions, I place an order on my father's behalf. Have the necessary sensitivity to treat and help people. They do not distinguish her by the color of her skin, the clothes she wears, her sex drive or even financial power. Treat everyone equally according to medical ethics and if it is within your reach, do not allow the omission with which many are treated. Do not blame the government for the poor health conditions because the government is made by people and feel part of it. So, play your role as a public servant or as a private employee.

"Behold, God gave gifts frequent to three of his servants. To one, he gave two talents. To others, three talents. To a third, four talents. The one who had four was stagnant and buried his talents. Those who had two and three worked in the vineyard and in the wheat field and expanded the boss's harvest. For this reason, God took the four talents from the lazy servant and gave them to others because whoever does not bear good fruit loses his father's grace."

The intrigue

Live in peace with yourself and with others. Avoid intrigue, as it is the flame that consumes the soul. Look for dialogue first and discussions, and useless intrigues will be avoided. If you cannot avoid the misunderstanding, surrender to God and pray for the opponent, as he is a person who needs help.

The tramp

Man has to work to achieve dignity. Regardless of the job, feel happy to play a role. On the contrary vagabonds eat from those who work and are a hindrance to society.

Never allow yourself to stand still. If you don't work, at least study and take your time. Idle mind is a danger that is where Satan works against the children of God. Think about it.

The evolution

The earth is a dimension of atonement and evidence, since we are spirits sent to learn and teach together with our fellow men. Everything we live here has a great purpose.

Our lives are made of joy and pain and both teach a lot. In happy moments, we share the victory with those we love and moments of pain and failure always lead us to a reflection of mistakes and successes. I believe that failure is the right catapult for us to get it right in the future and as a result, we learn more from it.

This set of factors gradually purifies us and gives us more experience to the point where we consider ourselves evolved. Getting to the bridge that takes us to the light is the main objective on this planet, that is, it is the law of return from where we came from. When we reach this grace, we will see that everything was very worthwhile between obstacles and experiences. However, nothing is by chance. If he got to the bridge, it was because he was worthy of it through his choices.

The friendship

Friendship is a rare jewel, whoever finds it has a real treasure. Try to make friends with people who are fun, ethical, honest, respectful and at ease with life. With the family, they will be your support in difficult times.

Be a real friend. Try to talk and understand others. Give advice, but respect the individuality of the other, as each is autonomous in their own decisions. Like a relationship, friendship has to be watered daily so that it remains and bear's fruit.

God encourages friendship between humans, but points out that many of them abandon at times when we need it most. If this happens to you, turn to him who is a loving and helpful father. In it, you will be able to surrender all your confidence.

Suffering for love

Love is the most sublime of feelings, but it is also the most terrible when we love without being reciprocated. In this situation, it is best to try to forget. This task will not be easy if you have frequent contact with your loved one, but do not give up. Give time to time, meet new people, stroll, spend your time with pleasurable activities.

The most important thing in all this is to value yourself and if the other person has rejected you, it is because you are not worthy of your love. Do not insist on something that didn't work out in the beginning, as it will only bring more suffering for both of you.

The day will come when you will no longer love a certain person, and then you will be free to decide how to go about your life. Try to start your love life over again, but cautiously, as no one is important enough to cause you more pain and tears. Think about it.

An attitude of life

I, as a servant and son of God the father, follow my own rules regarding living with others in society. I will cultivate love, respect, equality, charity, understanding, friendship by being loyal and sincere with everyone.

In dealing with the other, I will put myself in his place and never address offensive words that may hurt him. If I have to make a correction, I do it in a way that is a constructive criticism.

However, most do not mind stepping on, hurting and feeling superior to others. I have been a victim, countless times, of this destructiveness of the next, and I suffered in silence because I would never fight back violence with another violence. It may seem naive, but that's the way I am, and I feel happy about it.

Do as I do, make a difference and always promote good and peace.

The wounded marks

Wound marks are the sequels that we carry from all the pains imposed by life. Many sufferings are of such magnitude that they leave these marks permanently. How to live with them?

First, there must be a reflective and positive attitude towards life. Finding something to learn in suffering and trying to live his life independently. To seek inspiration in the various examples of martyrs who knew how to channel their pain to something greater and this point that I want to reach, channeling.

If we have a goal and fight for it, everything we live with is left behind. It is not a question of forgetting the problem, but of living in such a way that it cannot harm us. Trusting your faith in something or in a God also helps a lot in the healing of these marks.

Finally, never let suffering take over your actions completely. Go with your head up, and I sincerely hope that you are happy.

Being an eternal learner

Some ask me: how do you define yourself? I answer: "I am an eternal apprentice". It is this phrase that I take with me wherever I go. Even though I often play the role of a master, I am fully aware that I do not know everything and that the path is not yet ready.

Seeking his way with his ethics and effort is what man must do. However, the rule of humility and simplicity must always be followed if he wants success.

In social relations, never slander, judge or disparage others, as we are not perfect. How will a blind person guide another blind person? First remove the beam from your eye, so you can see better, and then you can give advice.

With these basic premises, humanity would advance in all aspects and many problems would be avoided. Always know how to discern the situation.

Advertising

Currently, there is an explosion of visual and graphic advertising using all available means. When the product is good or the cause is just, you have no problem wanting to publicize your work.

The biggest problem is when they want to impose on the consumer, products of dubious origin, offering illicit drugs, apology for racism, crime and rebellion, addressing controversial issues without justification. As a consumer, I abhor these situations and take the appropriate measures for my protection, as respect and quality are essential for good 'marketing'.

We will do our part by excluding from our social relationships the people and companies that use the power of communication to disturb and harm others. I'm counting on you!

Pornography and the trivialization of sex

The modern world as it stands has an abundance of deviations from what my father wants. The most serious faults are materialism, falsehood, competition without limits, disrespect, intolerance, lack of morals, pornography, and the trivialization of sex.

I will stick to the last two in this topic. With the explosion of virtual media, the demand for casual sex and pornography has only increased in recent years. A clear example of this is the chat rooms where most people are looking for a fleeting adventure. The danger lurks in several ways: contact with strangers, disclosure of personal data, lies that hurt the human heart, exposure, and discouragement to find people with such a poor soul except for rare exceptions. For this reason, the recommendations are as follows for those who access these virtual environments: do not trust anyone you do not know, do not give your full name, phone number, personal and work address. Marital status, e-mail, etc. Try to be as succinct as possible with strangers.

My father and I want servants who are clean in heart and soul. We do not accept sexual perversions such as prostitution, incest, pedophilia, pornography and casual sex. Value your body and make it a temple of the Holy Spirit. Love yourself more!

The value of a human being.

In my view and that of my father, all men are equal. Whether you are rich, poor, thin, fat, from any religion or belief, from any country, from any race or ethnicity, from any political, ideological and sexual option or any other group, my kingdom is open to everyone. I ask you only to follow my eternal laws recorded in the commandments of the old and new covenants.

By surrendering your life and your problems with confidence to the true God, you will be opening the doors for your action and then your life will be completely transformed. You will feel my love that is greater than anything you can imagine or understand. Then happiness will be a reality in your life.

The sublime role of the master.

You, who are a master in your field, never stop teaching. Always spread your talent for human development. Knows that your contribution is important for everyone who craves knowledge. Be sincere when the challenge is greater than your ability and learn from others as well. That is why we live in society, to help each other.

Be aware that those who teach here will one day shine like stars perpetuating their light and goodness. They will receive the fair reward for their efforts together with the apprentices.

Greatness in the little things

Each man was put on earth for a purpose. Big or small, they perform essential tasks for the proper ordering of the planet. So don't judge your work inferior, no matter how small. Greatness shows itself in small things and whoever is faithful in small things is also shown in big ones. So, cheer up and continue perpetuating the good in all your attitudes.

The pride

This is a sin responsible for the biggest obstacle in the evolution of the human being. When a man lets himself be dominated by his pride and self-sufficiency, he cannot see anything concrete that makes him happy. This feeling keeps you stuck in your misery. Man, human worm, wake up to reality. You can do nothing without the consent of the omnipotent, omnipresent and omniscient father. Everything here on earth is fleeting, including your life. You will only realize this when something happens to you or someone close to you. You will see how fragile the human being is always subject to accidents, diseases, urban and rural violence, misery, misunderstanding, and lack of love. Only the father's grace can sustain and save him.

Acknowledge your smallness, practice the commandments, do good without looking at whom, and then I will bless you. At this moment, pride was overcome by simplicity and humility. It is these two virtues that must always be carried on the chest.

Lust

Brothers, have a healthy sexuality. If you are married, live in a stable relationship or dating, have fidelity and loyalty as the main point. Respect those who are by your side and yourself by not having relationships with other people. Single, your freedom is relative. Live in a healthy way and get involved only with trusted people. Be cautious when having sex to prevent sexually transmitted diseases. Your life is unique and God wants to preserve it.

Do not allow yourself to practice or get involved with people who practice sexual abominations, such as Zoophilia, incest, pedophilia and other perversions. However, if any of these come to you asking for help, do not refuse to cooperate.

In conclusion, let us have a healthy sexual activity without compromising the spiritual side. Cultivate the ethics of goodness. As a certain friend said, act in a way that does not harm or make anyone suffer.

Greediness

Everything in this world has to have limits and reasonableness. The same is true of eating food and drink. Do not be carried away by selfishness, greed and eat only what is necessary to survive. By controlling your instincts, you will have the opportunity to take a clearer and safer path relates what God the Father wants. Use temperance and be happy with yourself.

Avarice

Avarice is a grave sin that leads the practitioner to a sea of sadness and loneliness. Valuing selfishness, a person distances himself from God and exchanged him for the value of material goods. Brothers, reflect and think! All material goods are of weak consistency and ephemeral. Therefore, there is no point in worshiping them.

We must value what really matters: God, first, love, family, and neighbor. In doing so, all things will be added to it and there will be no sin in it. Always think about the good of the other, fulfill your obligations, do charity and the sin you commit on earth can be forgiven and redeemed. Be more human, and then you can see the glory of God.

Will

Anger is a bad feeling that accompanies all violent people. Acting with unreasonable hatred, these people can physically and verbally attack others and even kill.

This indomitable beast has always haunted humanity and was the cause of countless tragedies. I believe that this category of reaction is part of human nature, but like any other orientation it can be changed.

Be guided by the example of Jesus, a faithful, meek and humble man, and do it differently. Respect, love and protect your neighbor as if it were with your parents or with God Himself. In doing so, peace and tranquility will surely reign in your life, and it is now that you will realize that hate or violence is not worth it.

Vanity

Vanity is an addiction that affects many people. Thinking only on the outside, these individuals strive to appear impeccable before society to provoke admiration and envy.

But I say to you: take care of your body, but avoid overdoing it. The most important thing about man is not his exterior, but focusing on the beneficial acts that make the interior more beautiful. In the end, it will not matter if you are thin, fat, beautiful, or ugly, what matters is your eternal soul. Therefore, try to keep the commandments of the old and new covenants and related themes, and you will achieve what you are looking for.

Laziness

Do not be overwhelmed by lack of motivation or the uncertainties of life. Always try to lift your head and follow because laziness is a bad sin that if it contaminates you, it can lead you to ruin.

Laziness leads to misery and the lack of dignity itself, not even your relatives will respect you. So, show what you are capable of: present yourself willing to face any category of situation and go to the fight wherever the war goes. With that, it will provoke the admiration of the next one, and it will not lose the battle before even having tried. Good luck to everyone!

Envy

Here is a silent worm that settles in most humans and wreaks havoc. Caring only for the lives of others, the envious person ceases to walk his path and is stagnant in time and in the space.

Try to live your life and strive to achieve your goals that God will bless you in due time. Everyone deserves success guaranteed and considering that do not worry about others. Do your part that will be all right because you are also a child of God. Have a positive attitude towards life.

The game

There are two forms of game that must be analyzed: The casual player who risks his luck once or another and continues to follow his obligations and the usual player who does not spend a week without playing. This guy can do anything to feed his addiction, including pawning personal valuables.

This second type is the most dangerous for the human being that leads to a degradation of his personal life. Even if you win sometimes, this only fuels your desire to gamble and usually comes a succession of defeats that bring you to ruin. One of my apostles in "I am" was a professional player and through group treatment he ended up overcoming his problems, which is a rarity. If you are a gambler or know someone who is, do not hesitate to seek specialized help, as it is pleasing to God for a human being without addictions. Do it differently and change your story or that of the other.

Drugs

The drug is another addiction that degrades the human being's life. Lawful or illicit, it impairs the functioning of the organism in its vital functions. Do not get carried away by fashion and do not try or use drugs. You will be a happier, healthier and more fulfilled human being.

Whoever uses or traffics drugs is usually involved in crime, such as street children who rob and kill to buy drugs. This is sacrilege to God! Instead, these boys should be studying or in recovery centers for drug addicts that it is the duty of society as a whole to maintain.

So, if you have someone in the family who is drugged, don't give up on him. Insist on getting it back in every way and if you can't do it alone, get help. Victory will be achieved and God the Father will bless you.

God seeks the faithful servant and to receive him we must be free from all material and spiritual drugs. Be pure and free. Be happy.

Posture at home

In my home, which is a simple and humble residence, I follow some basic rules of coexistence: equality between family members, respect, love, and understanding. Relates others, one thing I do not admit is the curse of others' lives and the opposite is common in many homes around the world. Guys, think about it. The other person's life is not about us, and we should only take care of our life, which already has its problems. So as Jesus said, do not judge, and you will not be judged. In the same measure that you judge, you will also have to account for your sins. What will they pay with? What does man have to offer in exchange for his soul? A reflection has to be made relates oneself, to the family, to God and to the neighbor? So, be careful with the ferocious tongue!

The greenhouse effect and its causes.

The greenhouse effect is a physical process that consists of when part of the infrared radiation emitted by the Earth's surface is absorbed by some gases present in the atmosphere. In the limits, this effect is beneficial, as it keeps the planet warm. However, several factors are contributing to the intensification of this process, generating the phenomenon known as global warming. Among the main ones are the burning of fossil fuels, the indiscriminate use of certain fertilizers, deforestation, and food waste.

The most well-known fossil fuels are mineral coal, oil and natural gas. Used as fuels, these elements produce about twenty-one billion tons of dioxide, with half of this production reaching the atmosphere. These numbers show the ecological and environmental risk that we are taking when using them because this aggravates the environmental issue and leaves us at the mercy of the growing warming.

Regarding fertilizers, we have two types that are used: organic and inorganic. The organic is made from natural products such as castor, humus, algae, and manure and contributes to the increase in the soil's biodiversity and its productivity. Already inorganic is made from chemical products and among its components are nitrogen, sulfur, magnesium, and potassium. As it has a greater productivity gain, it is used generally. However, the main consequences affect soil quality, water pollution and air pollution now dealt with. In evidence the greed of man to produce more, earn more money even without quality, putting everyone's life at risk.

The issue of deforestation is even more complicated in Brazil and in the world. Driven by the demographic explosion and urbanization, it is increasingly common to convert land from closed forest to land for pasture and agriculture, in addition to logging for the construction of furniture and general use, land grabbing and support for infrastructures such as civil construction. The relationship with the problem of worsening global warming is the fact that when a forest is cut down and burned, carbon is released, which contributes to the greenhouse effect. As this fact is inevitable and becomes more constant, the problem tends to worsen. These factors have already been widely debated by researchers and scholars in general. Some point to sustainable development to halt this process. In my opinion, it is a good alternative, and it is possible, but in contradiction there is the exacerbated industrial, demographic, and commercial growth making us live the dilemma of civilized man in opposition to development.

Another major problem is the waste of food that has already reached an impressive 1.3 billion tones according to FAO. This amount generates 3.3 billion tons of gases that affect the greenhouse effect in addition to a water expenditure equivalent to the annual flow of the Volga River in Russia. Given this scenario, what can be done as corrective measures are: priority in reducing food consumption, balancing the law of supply and demand; reuse food in a way that is not wasted and an emphasis on recycling.

That said, we see that there are many serious problems that make the greenhouse effect still an issue to be overcome. However, there is a possible path to follow. Each must do its part and demand a counterpart from governments. How to do your part? Using renewable materials, saving water, energy, not wasting food, recycling waste, buying products from companies with a quality seal in environmental management show a commitment to the environmental cause with a focus on sustainable development. We will make our planet a more pleasant place to live and that this will last for many, many generations. This is what God expects from human beings.

Trafficking in animals and plants.

There is a growing demand for trafficking in wild animals and plants, an activity that puts the biodiversity of our forests at risk. The motivations are many, ranging from the use of part of animals and plants in commercial products to the use of animals as pets, and use for collectors and zoos. This is a market in which it is estimated to move around twenty billion dollars.

Once again, the whole question is about money and the man with his exacerbated greed does not care to defraud and cause suffering in these small beings. In the face of a government that is often sluggish, we, as citizens, must denounce suspicious behavior and not condone this aggression to our natural heritage. We will contribute to a fairer and more dignified country. Save nature.

Landless movement, without food, homeless, etc.

These groups of people seek through an association to join the struggle by claiming their rights. This attitude is commendable, as everyone should have equal opportunities for development. It is written in the Brazilian Constitution in its sixth article: Education, health, food, work, housing, leisure, security, official social security, maternity protection, childhood, and assistance to the destitute are social rights.

What cannot be admitted is that these groups harm the lives of others in protests because our right ends when the others start. If you want to protest, you have every now to do so peacefully so that it does not harm anyone. Putting yourself in the other's shoes is beneficial and pleasing to God.

Capitalism

Capitalism is a predominant economic system in the western region of the world where the production processes are mostly concentrated in the hands of the private sector. Its other characteristics are wage labor, creation of products for profit and competitive prices. While it encourages economic growth, capitalism generates concentration of income and consequently social stratification and misery.

As my father's advisor, I just observe that there must be a greater appreciation of the worker with an extension of his rights and a greater respect for employers. The production process is a three-way street where raw materials, workers and financial capital must always go together. When success is achieved, it belongs to everyone. Furthermore, there is no reason for God to interfere in human production systems due to the question of free will.

Plastic surgeries due to vanity

Some people just looking to get prettier do incessant plastic surgery. However, many times, its interior remains ugly and dirty. My brothers realize that the outside is not relevant, that you will grow old and your beauty will pass. Try to take care of your soul in the first place, whether by working, helping others in deeds and words. It is his works that will define his eternal future and if he is good, you will achieve true happiness.

It is not forbidden to take care of your body or perform surgical procedures due to your health and well-being, but performing surgery just for vanity is a big waste of time.

Abortion

Abortion is the purposeful removal of a fetus from a human uterus and according to Brazilian legislation, it is classified as a crime against life with a forecast of detention ranging from one to ten years depending on the case. A very controversial topic, it has been debated constantly in the highest instances of the courts. By law, it is disqualified as a crime in three situations: when there is a risk of life for the pregnant woman, when the pregnancy occurs due to a rape.

In God's view, life is sacred regardless of the situation. So, if it is possible for the baby and the mother to survive together then it must be accepted by the one who generated it. God disapproves of the conduct of abortion in general and of people who have babies and simply discard it. If they were responsible enough to have a sexual relationship, they must also be responsible with the generated being, who is an innocent person who needs protection and love.

In the reverse of history, the practice of contraceptives and condoms that protect partners in a relationship cannot be considered a sin as some Churches emphasize. The family and their upbringing are the couple's responsibility, and only they are in charge of finding out how many children they can raise. They thus contribute to avoid an overpopulation which would be a major factor in a major crisis on Earth. As for the condom, in addition to the factor, birth, it is an important ally in the prevention of sexually transmitted diseases.

Pedophilia

It is a disorder of sexual preference for children (male or female) or at the beginning of puberty. It is a very disapproved attitude by my father, as they must be respected and preserved in their innocence.

Pedophiles are sick people who should seek treatment. It is useless to want to judge or condemn them, but to seek help in their healing process. Although difficult, recovery is fully possible. I chose a pedophile to be my apostle in the fifth book in the series "The Seer" entitled "I am". The objective was to show that everyone deserves a second chance and should not be prejudiced especially in the case of pedophilia because it is a disease.

Zoophilia

It is a sexual disorder defined by the attraction or sexual involvement of humans with animals of another species. It is also an attitude widely disapproved of by my father.

Man was made to relate affectionately to another pair of the same species and does not need to look for an animal to satisfy himself. This is a serious misconduct, classified as a disease and as such requires treatment. Like the pedophile, he has the possibility to recover and for that, he needs all the support of his family and friends.

Incest

It is sexual practice with family members or close relatives. It is another prohibitive sexual practice for my father. Family relationships should only be about companionship and mutual support without involving sexuality.

The man or woman should look for a partner outside their family context, as blood cannot mix with their blood. This is an eternal law that must be followed and that is also part of ethics.

Prostitution

Brothers, your body is a temple of the Holy Spirit; therefore, we must take care to keep it pure and clean. Whoever prostitutes himself loses the respect of society and of himself. Thus, it becomes anybody.

We must value ourselves by doing right. Never accept perversion for money, as this is blasphemy against God. Your soul is the most important thing that you have to preserve.

Jesus' example of not condemning Mary shows that the past no longer matters. It is possible to change and repent of your sins. If you are in prostitution, change your attitude and become a son of God.

Adultery

Adultery is having a partner, spouse and relating to other people. Attitude disapproved by God, leads the human being to a dangerous and conflicting "Dark night of the soul".

It is better not to marry or make a commitment than to be in communion and cheating at the same time. This category of attitude destroys the trust that is the most important that the couple can have with each other. It is up to the betrayed to weigh the possibilities and decide what would affect his happiness.

In addition to a conjugal sin, it is a sin against God and against the family. The adulterer only has to repent and trust in divine mercy because his situation is really complicated. However, change is always possible and everyone deserves opportunities for reconciliation.

Sexual Orientations

A person's sexual orientation can vary between heterosexuality, bisexuality, homosexuality, asexual, and pansexuality. This is believed to be due to genetic factors and therefore there is no scope for choice.

Man is what is born and must assume and be respected for it. It does not matter the sexuality of the man, but his character. The belief that God abhors homosexuality is unfounded. What is written in some books did not come out of God because know him because he is my father. All prejudice is of human origin only. My father is looking for faithful servants in all nations and requires only a commitment to their causes. So, have more faith, brothers and live your sexuality in a healthy way. Do not restrain yourself because you will not be condemned for it.

Behold, there will be a time in the future land where humans will love each other freely. We will have couples of homosexuals, heterosexuals, asexual, bisexuals and pansexual living in harmony. On this day, which will be the day of God, tolerance and love will definitely overcome prejudice.

Scientific research with humans and animals.

Scientific research involving human beings and animals must follow a logical ethics that respects the rights of the person being examined. Relate experiments with humans, there is a set of guidelines (International ethical guidelines for research involving human beings) to be followed and the main one is the subject's consent or the legal representative who authorizes the research. This with an ample explanation of the risks to which he runs. Once these steps have been completed, there is nothing to question about being supported by the free will of both.

Relates the experiment with animals, one should try to avoid their suffering as much as possible and provide adequate food and facilities, as their use in projects is often indispensable in the search for alternative treatments and cures for various diseases. Man is the center of creation and the use of animals to help him does not prove to be contrary to divine laws, since everything was given to him by his father.

The use of stem cells, the use of artificial insemination and in vitro fertilization.

The use of stem cells is a modern method of medicine to treat various problems and diseases of man. However, its use has been the subject of much controversy and discussions by religious, politicians, lay people, in short, all sectors of society.

My position is this: when the stem cell is removed from the patient's own body and will help him to treat his health by giving him relief and the prospect of survival, why not use it? Let us leave prejudices aside and see that this method really has its value in the treatment of cancer, Alzheimer's disease, heart disease, Parkinson's disease, spinal cord trauma, heart attack, burns, diabetes, osteoarthritis, rheumatoid arthritis, among others. What I disagree with is the generation of embryos for this purpose and cloning. There the human being is already immersed in the field of creation, which represents a great danger.

Relative to artificial insemination and in vitro fertilization, its use is providing several previously infertile couples to have children. The objective is noble and even if the methods are not justified, we can say they are acceptable. This aspect is adverse with the religious side, but as a representative of God I can say that there is no condemnation for that.

Current public health

We live in a very complicated situation in public health. Resources are lacking and what we have is poorly applied, generating immediate consequences for the population with lower purchasing power. It is common the lack of doctors in general, of medicines and basic materials, overcrowding of ICUs (intensive care units), neglect of care, causing many to die.

With each new election, promises of improvement come, but traditionally, the problems remain and worsen. What to do? In addition to the power of choice during universal suffrage, we can demand our rights as a citizen by working in community groups that oversee the government and even go to court. We fulfill our duties by paying various taxes and fees. Therefore, we are entitled to at least decent health. We will make Brazil a better country, leaders, and representatives of society.

Public education

This is another area in which Brazil needs to improve a lot in every way. The main aspects of the reform are: a greater allocation of resources by the government, greater supervision in the application of these resources, a teacher qualification program, an improvement in the salaries of professionals, a more adequate and more assorted teaching material, basic infrastructure equipment, security, investment in science and technology, among others.

If everything is fulfilling to the letter, we will have an education from acceptable to good. With scientific, technological, economic development and the consequent generation of jobs, our country has every possibility to stand out worldwide, because we have human material for this. The Brazilian is the nation's greatest wealth.

Corruption

I have a message from my father to the managers in general. You have entrusted the control, coordination and effectiveness of the projects with a view to the common well-being. If you rebel and act for your own benefit, you are certainly tracing a path that will end with the mansion of the dead. There, there will be weeping and gnashing of teeth in order to pay the debt for sin.

Remember that you will take nothing from this earthly to the spiritual world except your own works. Therefore, make an effort to maintain transparency, rectitude and honesty with the public thing, which is your obligation as a representative of the people. Make a difference by transforming the lives of the little ones for the better through your actions and I will bless you and give you many years of life.

Safety

The contemporary world reveals a world of uncertainty for the citizen in almost all the world. Violence is everywhere haunting the good citizen and it seems to me that public efforts in this area are not having much effect. Assault, fraud, scam, fraud, physical and verbal aggression have become so common that victims do not even bother to press charges. What to do in the face of such a catastrophic reality?

First of all, it is necessary to reformulate the penal code, which is very broad, with stricter penalties for situations that are necessary, thus inhibiting the practice of crime. In addition, it is necessary to reinsert the prisoner into society when it is possible through serious public policies and programs. Most of the time, prejudice and rejection reign with newly released prisoners. Other important measures are: reduction of economic and social inequality, valorization of civil servants linked to this area and greater clarification of the population in relation to their own preventive measures.

Peace and tranquility are possible one day if there is a big joint effort by society and government. We will punish the guilty, give them a second chance by reinserting them in society and, if they repeat, act firmly in the law, because there is no place in the community or in the kingdom of God for those who seek the unique purpose of harming others. God seeks the just and the good.

Strike

The strike is a right guaranteed by law to all categories of workers who seek fairer working conditions. In legal terms, which guarantees the performance of the service in thirty percent (essential), the worker has every right to speak up and demand improvements.

It is a great negotiation tool between strikers and employers and often achieves important advances for the public service and the quality of life of the server in general. Therefore, every strike is valid and essential in the fight for rights.

Live the present

Enjoy every important moment of your life. Live the present in such a way that there is no future. It is the rare moments of happiness that make life worth living.

Don't worry about your past or what's to come. Try to do good today so you can feel fulfilled. Go on with your life always with optimism, perseverance and faith.

The suicide

Trying to destroy your own life is a serious sin against God. We must continue with our mission regardless of the results and consequences, as this is to be a winner. Surrendering is definitely not the best solution for anyone.

People who seek to end their lives are often experiencing a deep depression that must be dealt with. With the advice of professionals and the help of friends it is possible to reverse the situation and the person will return to normal life. Living on earth is a gift from God and cannot, under any circumstances, be wasted.

Depression

Depression is a problem that plagues more and more people. Taken as a modern disease, it causes the victim to lose heart completely, often generating serious consequences. It is usually triggered for some reason: a love disappointment, a professional frustration, a major loss, a betrayal, among others.

Treatment for depression ranges from follow-up with a psychologist to medication administration depending on the case. In milder cases, a good conversation will do. If you experience any symptoms of persistent discouragement, do not hesitate to seek the help of a professional. The sooner the better. Take care of yourself and be happy.

Drug trafficking

This activity consists of the commercialization of substances that are considered illegal by the governments. In general, trafficking is linked to crime and subversion. It is estimated that this trade moves values higher than spending on food.

In my view and that of my father, the human being has no need to resort to any category of drugs to feel happy, more courageous or fulfilled. Happiness comes from personal achievements and it is not a physical effect. Therefore, drugs should be avoided and efficient means of repression should be placed on their commercialization in order to avoid their consumption. For a world without drugs and violence, amen!

Trafficking in persons

It is the trade in human beings recruited mostly for sexual purposes, forced labor and organ harvesting. Moving tens of billions of dollars, a year, it is one of the fastest growing criminal activities.

As it is a violation of human rights, it is constantly condemned by international conventions and also by my father.

Whoever practices this crime is in a complicated situation in spiritual and civil terms.

What must be done in these cases is preventive and repressive work that makes it difficult for criminals to act. Preventive refers to being wary of proposals from strangers mainly regarding lucrative jobs abroad and repressive in terms of not being afraid to report suspicious cases. In addition to making people aware of not looking for the services offered by these vandals. If people are not interested, the demand for trafficking will be much lower.

Together we can combat this evil of society, which is an affront to a so-called organized society. Every human being is free to make his choices and have work and dignity. Therefore, I condemn human trafficking.

Greed

Try to take care of your own life and do not want for yourself what belongs to the other. Each one has only what he deserves and wait patiently, as his turn will come and then he will be able to enjoy the fruits of his own work.

There is no magic formula for success. You need to have focus, dedication, good planning, competence, perseverance, patience and faith. The obstacles that come along the way serve to strengthen us and make us fit for big victories. God wants the good of all and will bless his efforts in due time.

The mission

"Behold, I am sending you out as sheep among wolves. Therefore, be prudent as serpents and simple as doves. Be careful with men.

This message from Jesus addressed to the apostles shows fundamental advice for all Christians and that extends to other denominations: The vast majority of the world is composed of wickedness and rebellion and as a result, we must be careful with our actions and words. This is not cowardice and a precautionary measure so that we can have a bearable and healthy coexistence with groups with interests different from ours.

Respect and tolerance are also fundamental to maintaining peace and harmony. Let us be like Jesus, simple and humble in heart and through the right elements we will be able to conquer the world with our example. It will be a great achievement, as many people and denominations prefer to conquer goals through strength and this only increases, insecurity, and violence. Let us do it differently and be true apostles of the bodily son of God.

Recognize yourself a sinner

All human beings are imperfect, there is not even one perfect. Therefore, let us recognize our faults, cling to the forces of heaven and put on a new man. Transformed by the power of light, we will be able to win the battle against our darkness.

Do not have pride, vanity, anger, envy or any feeling of self-sufficiency, as we are weak and dependent on the grace of the father. It is precisely in weakness that strength and proof of my infinite love and my fathers for humanity are produced. Considering that, faith brothers, you are worth a lot!

The spiritual dimensions

Most people still have doubts about the afterlife and the spiritual dimensions. Heaven, hell, city of men and purgatory are some so-called consciences of souls. This is because these plans are not about physical places, but spiritual states.

Therefore, in flesh or spirit, man lives with his reality according to his evolution. The dimensions are in us. Considering this, let us make today our path to the path of goodness and take advantage of heaven right here on earth.

The disabled

Disabled people are special people very much loved by the father who must be treated with love and respect for everyone. Depending on the problem they have, they are fully capable of working, going out, taking a walk and having a normal life.

Being disabled is not a shame for anyone. What is shameful is cruelty, criminality, falsehood, and malice in general. It is important to note that most of the deficiencies are genetic and my father cannot be held responsible for this. It is more common to attribute nature to more justice.

To the disabled, live your life with peace and joy, be a servant of God and your disability does not leave you with less merit. They just make it special. It is your attitudes and works that will define your destiny.

The value of culture

Brazilian culture is diverse and composed of different aspects which were responsible for the formation of our population: the black, the Indian, and the white. We thus have an immense wealth to share with the world.

Value and encourage culture in its entirety. Give yourself this leisure as a gift to yourself: go to the cinema, the theater, the circus, a stadium, read a book in the tranquility of your home. It will certainly be of great value to your life, as acquiring wisdom is critical.

Do not be afraid

You are a child of God and very much loved by the father. Feel happy for the gift of life. Even if the challenges and problems are huge, face them with courage, perseverance, and faith. It is entirely possible to win. Just don't give in and don't be afraid to take chances.

The father and mother as family axes.

The father and the mother must be the mainstay of the house in the financial, emotional, spiritual and moral aspects. In return, children must be obedient and loving. It is a mutual exchange between them that will take place until the end of life.

In old age, the protection and care of children are essential for the elderly to rest in peace. It is more than just because when we were young, we were cared for by them. So, remember that and don't be ungrateful to your parents.

Reasonability and proportionality

Reasonability and proportionality must be considered in all your activities on the land. Using them, the human being saves useless efforts and keeps the focus on the essentials.

Effectiveness, justice, good analysis, patience, and fidelity are also important, as these build a suitable, warlike and winning personality. Good luck to everyone in your endeavors.

Despise selfishness

Whatever you have to do, make him happy for of the other. Avoiding selfishness, one of the great virtues that God appreciates flourishes in the soul: Magnanimity. This is the meaning of life: to serve others and the universe without expecting a counterpart.

Without even realizing it, your projects and dreams will come true because God blesses you. In the future kingdom, you will have a special place with my father and me and nothing will happen to you during your stay on Earth. We need to change the stereotype of inhumanity and indifference that stands out in people by being a perfect apostle of the risen Christ. However, to do so, you must be aware of your generous role in the lives of everyone around you. Considering this, do not hesitate. Always do good with detachment.

In victory and failure

Enjoy every moment of your life. Make the brief moments as important as you can because time is fleeting. No one will take anything from this land except his works and the happiness he has enjoyed.

Always remember: in victory or failure, remain strong and strong in spirit. Your success and happiness depend on your strength. Never discredit the infinite power and love of your father who is in heaven. Make this title of "Son of God" stand out by planting good seeds and spreading joy and comfort wherever you go.

Be true light

"I was walking in a deserted place suffocated by intense shadows that were chasing me. As I did a good deed, my inner light grew stronger and gradually drove away the darkness. At the end of the path, they disappeared completely".

This elegant phrase contains the meaning of being a Christian. We are sheep among wolves that want to consume us. To face them, we must continue with our good deeds in such a way that the evil no longer affects us. The more you strive, the more results you will reap according to the maximum retribution.

End

www.ingramcontent.com/pod-product-compliance
Lightning Source LLC
LaVergne TN
LVHW020439080526
838202LV00055B/5260